Secrets of Our Sporting Heroes

Jill Bryant

Secrets of Our Sporting Heroes

Text: Jill Bryant
Publishers: Tania Mazzeo and Eliza Webb
Series consultant: Amanda Sutera
   Hands on Heads Consulting
Editor: Holly Proctor
Project editors: Annabel Smith and Jarrah Moore
Designer: Leigh Ashforth
Project designer: Danielle Maccarone
Permissions researcher: Liz McShane
Production controller: Renee Tome

Acknowledgements
We would like to thank the following for permission to reproduce
copyright material:

Front cover, p. 11: Alamy Stock Photo/ZUMA Press, Inc. Cover usage with
approval from Matt Formston, https://www.instagram.com/
mattformston; pp. 1, 5 (top right), 21 (top right): Alamy Stock Photo/Belga
News Agency; pp. 4, 8 (bottom): AFL Photos/Dylan Burns; pp. 5 (top left),
19 (top): Getty Images/Robert Gauthier; pp. 5 (middle left), 12 (bottom):
Getty Images/Matt Roberts/Stringer; pp. 5 (bottom), 27 (bottom): Getty
Images/Vaughn Ridley; p. 6 (top): Alamy Stock Photo/PA Images, (bottom):
Getty Images/Chris Hyde; p. 7: Alamy Stock Photo/UK Sports Pics Ltd; p. 8
(top): AAP Image/Joel Carrett; p. 9 (top): AFL Photos/Daniel Pockett,
(bottom): Newspix/John Feder ; p. 10: Getty Images/Robyn Beck; p. 11
(bottom): Getty Images/Robyn Beck; p. 12 (top): Getty Images/Alex
Davidson; ; p. 13 (top): Alamy Stock Photo/Mark Davidson, (bottom):
Alamy Stock Photo/PA Images; p. 14: Alamy Stock Photo/Action Plus
Sports Images; p. 15 (left): Alamy Stock Photo/dpa picture alliance, (right):
Getty Images/Dave Rowland; p. 16: Getty Images/Dario Belingheri; p. 17:
Alamy Stock Photo/Casey B. Gibson; p. 18: Alamy Stock Photo/UPI; p. 19
(bottom): Getty Images/Angelo Merendino; p. 20 (top): Shutterstock.
com/Leonard Zhukovsky, (bottom): Alamy Stock Photo/Andre Paes; p. 21
(bottom): Getty Images/Houston Chronicle/Hearst Newspapers via Getty
Images; p. 22: Shutterstock.com/Salty View; p. 23 (top): Alamy Stock
Photo/UPI; pp. 23 (bottom), 32: Alamy Stock Photo/Allstar Picture Library;
p. 24 (top): Alamy Stock Photo/Action Plus Sports Images, (bottom): Alamy
Stock Photo/DPPI Media; p. 25 (top): Alamy Stock Photo/NurPhoto SRL,
(bottom): Alamy Stock Photo/The Canadian Press; p. 26 (top): Alamy Stock
Photo/Orange Pics BV, (bottom): Getty Images/Matt Winkelmeyer; p. 27
(top): Alamy Stock Photo/dpa picture alliance; p. 28 (top): Getty
Images/Xavier Laine, (bottom): Getty Images/Hannah Foslien; p. 29: Getty
Images/Chris Tanouye/Freestyle Photo; p. 30, back cover: iStock.
com/SolStock.

Every effort has been made to trace and acknowledge copyright.
However, if any infringement has occurred, the publishers tender their
apologies and invite the copyright holders to contact them.

NovaStar

Text © 2024 Cengage Learning Australia Pty Limited

Cengage Learning Australia
Level 5, 80 Dorcas Street
Southbank VIC 3006 Australia
Phone: 1300 790 853
Email: aust.nelsonprimary@cengage.com

For learning solutions, visit cengage.com.au

Printed in China by 1010 Printing International Ltd
1 2 3 4 5 6 7 28 27 26 25 24

*Nelson acknowledges the Traditional Owners and Custodians
of the lands of all First Nations Peoples. We pay respect
to Elders past and present, and extend that respect to
all First Nations Peoples today.*

Contents

Ways to Win

It's easy to admire winning athletes. A look at 12 sporting stars from around the world reveals how they keep achieving great things. Despite challenges, these highly skilled athletes score goals, rack up points and land difficult jumps. They master waves, smash records and cross the finish line first.

- ⭐ How do these athletes do it?
- ⭐ What does it take to win and break records?
- ⭐ Do star athletes have superpowers?

Find out how they stay at the top of their game, in sport and in life.

Jamarra Ugle-Hagan

LeBron James

Madison de Rozario

Simone Biles

Yusra Mardini

Dylan Alcott

Date of birth → 1990

Place of birth →
Melbourne, Australia

Sport → wheelchair
tennis and basketball

Dylan celebrates victory in the men's quads wheelchair tennis singles at the 2021 Wimbledon Championships in England.

Dylan Alcott was a teenager with a lot of dreams who quickly found his **passion**. At age 17, he played for Australia at the 2008 Beijing Paralympics on the wheelchair basketball team. Dylan and his team won. At the 2012 London Paralympics, he and his teammates won a silver medal.

Dylan (left) plays wheelchair basketball at the 2009 Paralympic World Cup in Manchester.

6

Amazingly, Dylan was also a great tennis player. He first picked up a tennis racket in 2014, when he was 23. A year later, he'd won a staggering eight tennis **championships**. Then he took home two gold medals in the men's singles and doubles events at the 2016 Rio de Janeiro Paralympics. Dylan's accomplishments earned him the 2022 Australian of the Year award.

But Dylan was achieving great things off the tennis court, too. In 2018, he started a music festival called Ability Fest. Dylan has made sure that everyone feels welcome at the festival. It has ramps, elevators and paths for wheelchairs.

Although Dylan **retired** from tennis in 2022, he continues to encourage kids of all abilities to do their best and follow their passion!

Dylan plays in the men's quad wheelchair singles final at the 2020 Australian Open.

Jamarra Ugle-Hagan

Date of birth → 2002

Place of birth → Framlingham Aboriginal Reserve, Victoria, Australia

Sport → Australian Rules football

Jamarra Ugle-Hagan is an Indigenous Australian known for playing in the Australian Football **League** (AFL). He was raised on an Aboriginal **reserve** in western Victoria. Jamarra played football in a local competition, until he received an offer of a high school **football scholarship** at a private school far from his home. Jamarra was uncertain about leaving his supportive family, but he eventually accepted. It was a chance to focus on football and improve his skills.

Jamarra plays in an Australian Rules football match for the Western Bulldogs in 2023.

In 2020, Jamarra was the first footballer to be selected by an AFL team in the yearly **draft**. Since then, he tries his best to score goals for his team, the Western Bulldogs.

On 25 March 2023, 20-year-old Jamarra, a proud Indigenous athlete, acted against **racism**. Standing on the football field, he lifted his **guernsey** and pointed to his skin. It was a powerful moment. Almost 30 years before, another Indigenous AFL player named Nicky Winmar had done the same. Like Nicky, Jamarra believes in calling out racism.

Jamarra points to his skin as he celebrates kicking a goal during an AFL match in 2023.

Again and again, Jamarra proves he's one to watch.

Nicky Winmar bares his chest to supporters of the opposite team at an AFL match in 1993.

Matt Formston

Being Fearless

Date of birth → 1978

Place of birth → Sydney, Australia

Sport → adaptive surfing and para-cycling

Twelve-metre-high waves don't scare **adaptive surfer** Matt Formston. They excite him. Matt began his sporting career as a para-cyclist, representing Australia at the 2016 Rio de Janeiro Paralympics. In 2017, he began surfing professionally.

Matt is **visually impaired**, but with his amazing skills, Matt can "feel" a wave with his feet as he rides down it on his surfboard. A **sighted guide** tells him when a big wave is about to break. That's how Matt knows when to try and catch it.

Matt competes at the 2017 World Para Surfing Championship in California, the USA.

When Matt was growing up, some doctors and teachers told him he wouldn't be able to try sports. But they had no idea how fearless he could be on a surfboard!

Matt has earned the title of World Champion Adaptive Surfer three times! Now his dream is to surf in the Paralympic Games.

With his ability to set a goal and go for it, Matt inspires others to face their fears and try new challenges.

Matt competes at the 2022 World Para Surfing Championship in California, the USA.

Madison de Rozario

Setting Big Goals

Date of birth → 1993

Place of birth →
   Perth, Australia

Sport →
   wheelchair racing

What a force! From short sprints to long marathons, Madison de Rozario has done it all. She has competed at the Paralympics in Beijing in 2008, London in 2012, Rio de Janeiro in 2016 and Tokyo in 2021. She has won two gold medals, three silvers and a bronze.

At age 12, Madison began playing wheelchair basketball. She enjoyed it, but she wasn't sure if it was the best sport for her. After a while, the team's coach suggested she try racing. It was an instant fit! Madison had found her groove.

Madison races to the finish line to win gold in the women's T54 marathon at the 2018 Commonwealth Games in the Gold Coast, Australia.

Madison (left) wins the 2023 women's wheelchair race at the London Marathon.

From then on, Madison tried hard to improve her racing skills and overall fitness. She set big goals and stuck to a tough training **schedule**. In fact, Madison was only 14 at her first Paralympic Games.

Now a world champion racer and world record holder, Madison is an inspiring role model who keeps on winning.

Madison smiles after winning a bronze medal at the 2017 World Para Athletics Championships in London.

Valerie Adams

Having Strength and Courage

Date of birth → 1984

Place of birth → Rotorua, Aotearoa New Zealand

Sport → shot-put

Valerie Adams was always tall. At age 12, she towered above her classmates. She was good at basketball, but at age 13, **shot-put** captured her interest. Valerie's height and explosive strength helped her to throw the heavy metal ball a long way. She quickly broke her school's shot-put record!

However, Valerie's family couldn't afford new athletics shoes for her. So, at her first local competition, Valerie stood barefoot and courageous on the grass, preparing to throw. Again, she broke a record. Then, at age 14, she finished tenth at the World Youth Championships.

Yet this was only the beginning. After lots of hard training, Valerie competed for her country on the world stage. She went to five Olympic Games, winning gold medals at Beijing in 2008 and London in 2012. She took home a silver medal in Rio de Janeiro in 2016 and a bronze in Tokyo in 2021.

Valerie competes at the shot-put final at the Tokyo Olympic Games in 2021.

In 2022, Valerie retired from competition. She continues to be respected by many for her achievements in sport.

Valerie poses at the opening of a film about her life in 2022.

Niamh
Fisher-Black

Taking Risks

Date of birth → 2000

Place of birth →
Nelson, Aotearoa
New Zealand

Sport → cycling

Bike racing hasn't always been a smooth ride for Niamh (say: *Neev*) Fisher-Black. Since 2019, she has trained hard as a **professional** cyclist, on a professional cycling team. But unexpected challenges kept popping up. From late 2019 to 2023, the global Covid-19 **pandemic** slowed travel and disrupted cycling races. Then, when racing started again, Niamh's beloved cycling team wasn't able to continue. The reason? A lack of money for travelling and competing.

Niamh tried not to panic. She thought about what to do and chose a new cycling team wisely. Training with stronger riders pushed her to go faster and improve her cycling skills.

In 2022, Niamh had another setback. She found out she wouldn't receive any **funding** to travel to Australia for the World Championships. Could she miss the race? No way! She took a risk and decided to pay her own way.

In the end, it was worth it. Niamh was the first cyclist under 23 to finish the race. What an accomplishment!

Niamh is in the lead at the 2022 Road Cycling World Championships in Australia.

Niamh (centre, wearing black) competes in the women's under-23 road race at the 2022 Road Cycling World Championships in Australia.

LeBron James

Date of birth → 1984

Place of birth → Akron, USA

Sport → basketball

As a child, basketball star LeBron James and his mother didn't have much money and struggled to find a home. Sometimes they stayed with neighbours; other times with friends. Some days, LeBron saw fighting and street crime. But his mum always made sure he had food, clothing and a safe place to live.

At age nine, LeBron was skipping school a lot. His mother sent him to live with a kind-hearted football coach. She hoped that a regular schedule would help LeBron to stay at school. It did. LeBron started going to school more often. He also joined the basketball team. As the school's star player, he was called "King James". By the time he had finished high school, LeBron was a professional basketball player.

LeBron plays for his team the Los Angeles Lakers in 2023.

Fast-forward 20 years and LeBron is a superstar, on and off the basketball court. He speaks up for children's **rights**, donates money to school breakfast programs and pays to send young people to school. LeBron's generosity has a positive impact on kids who are struggling in different areas of life.

LeBron speaks at the LeBron James Family Foundation, which he created to help young people in his home town of Akron, USA.

Simone Biles

Putting Wellbeing First

Date of birth → 1997

Place of birth → Columbus, USA

Sport → gymnastics

As a young gymnast, Simone Biles didn't think she would go on to achieve anything special. But she rose to fame quickly, becoming an international gymnastics superstar. In fact, many people call her the greatest gymnast of all time. Simone earned an Olympic gold medal — not once, not twice, but four times at the Rio de Janeiro Olympics in 2016!

Simone competes on the beam at the 2016 Rio de Janeiro Olympics for Team USA.

However, during practice at the Tokyo Olympics in 2021, Simone experienced what gymnasts call the "twisties". She lost track of which way was up while spinning in the air. This caused Simone to feel worried, and she questioned her abilities. Bravely, she decided to put her personal wellbeing first and pulled out of several events. This decision earned her great support from the public. Later on in the competition, when she felt more at ease, she competed in one event and earned an Olympic bronze medal.

Simone performs on the uneven bars at the Artistic Gymnastics World Championships in Belgium in 2023.

Simone showed the world that taking care of your wellbeing is important. Other athletes and people around the world agreed.

Simone inspires many people to take care of their own health and wellbeing.

Usain Bolt

Trying Your Best

Date of birth → 1986

Place of birth →
   Montego Bay, Jamaica

Sport → sprinting

As a young kid in Jamaica,
Usain Bolt loved sports
like cricket and soccer. Then he tried
running. At age 15, he competed in the 2002 World Junior
Championships. He won a gold medal in the 200-metre sprint.

Later, in 2008, Usain competed at the Olympic Games in
Beijing. At the 2009 World Championships in Berlin, Germany,
he smashed the world record for the 100-metre sprint,
finishing in 9.58 seconds. He competed in Olympic Games
again at the 2012 London and 2016 Rio de Janeiro Olympics.
At all three Olympic Games, he earned gold medals
in the 100- and 200-metre sprints.

Usain wins the men's 100-metre sprint final at the 2016 Rio de Janeiro Olympics.

For Usain, success is about doing better. At a race in 2017, he had a poor start. Most sprinters would think their race was over. But Usain knew he could improve. He ran even faster, used his skills and won the race!

Off the track, Usain helps to improve the lives of Jamaican kids. He shares inspiring tips and donates sports equipment and laptops to schools. He loves encouraging kids to run hard, smile and do their best.

Usain Bolt often strikes a "lightning bolt" pose after a race.

Lydia Ko

Date of birth → 1997

Place of birth → Seoul, South Korea

Sport → golf

Lydia lifts her trophy at the New Zealand Women's Open in 2015.

Lydia Ko started playing golf when she was just five years old. Her rise to stardom was swift. In 2011, at age 14, she won a professional golf event in Australia. By 2013, she'd become a professional golfer. In 2015, at age 17, Lydia was the youngest golfer ever to be number one in the world.

In professional golf, winners earn cash prizes, sometimes over a million dollars! But for Lydia, winning isn't everything. Enjoying the game is just as important.

Lydia competes at a golfing championship in France in 2017.

Lydia plays a shot at the 2022 Women's World Championship in Singapore.

When she can take a Saturday off to relax, Lydia loves playing golf with her husband. She understands it's important to take it easy and enjoy life. Lydia never takes her professional wins for granted.

While competing, Lydia can feel nervous. But then she remembers fun-loving Saturday golf games and copies the same attitude. Enjoying the moment helps her keep calm.

Lydia smiles and keeps calm during the final round of the 2015 Canadian Pacific Women's Open golf tournament.

Yusra **Mardini**

Swimming for Hope

Date of birth → 1998

Place of birth → Damascus, Syria

Sport → swimming

Swim for your life? A competitive swimmer would never expect to have to do this. Yet that's exactly what Yusra Mardini and her sister Sara had to do.

Fleeing from war in Syria in 2015, Yusra and Sara huddled in an overcrowded boat with a broken motor. To save themselves and the other **refugees**, the sisters jumped into the sea. They swam and swam, towing the flimsy boat behind them. After three hours, they reached shore.

Yusra (right) and her sister Sara pose at the opening of a film about their experience, in 2022.

Settling in Germany, Yusra and Sara struggled to build a new life. Yusra's dream was to compete in the Olympic Games, but now she had no home country or team. Before long, her skills as a swimmer attracted attention. She was invited to join the Refugee Olympic Team. She accepted, thinking she could give other refugees hope.

Yusra takes a break during a training session in Berlin, Germany, in 2016.

Yusra competed at the Olympics at Rio de Janeiro in 2016 and Tokyo in 2021. When she won a race in Rio de Janeiro, the whole world celebrated. Yusra's inspiring story is one of bravery, respect and hope.

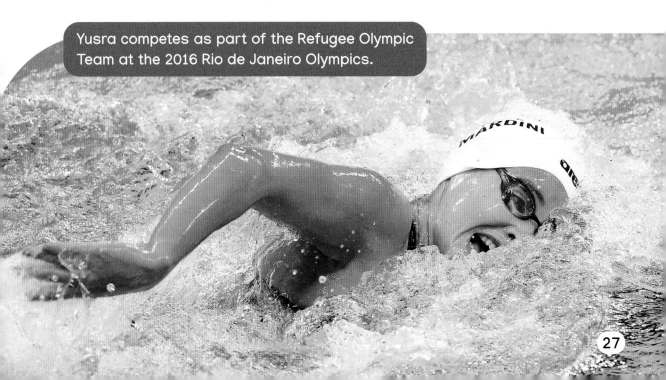

Yusra competes as part of the Refugee Olympic Team at the 2016 Rio de Janeiro Olympics.

Sarah Nurse

Improving Sport for Girls and Women

Date of birth → 1995

Place of birth →
  Hamilton, Canada

Sport → ice hockey

Sarah holds up her gold medal at the 2022 Beijing Olympics.

When ice hockey player Sarah Nurse scored five goals at the 2022 Beijing Winter Olympics, Canadian fans were astonished. It had been 16 years since an ice hockey player had shown such goal-shooting power. Sarah said scoring at the Olympic Games felt like magic. And it helped her team to win a gold medal! This win was even more special because of all of the hard work Sarah and her teammates had done in the years leading up to it.

Sarah plays against the USA team during a game in 2017.

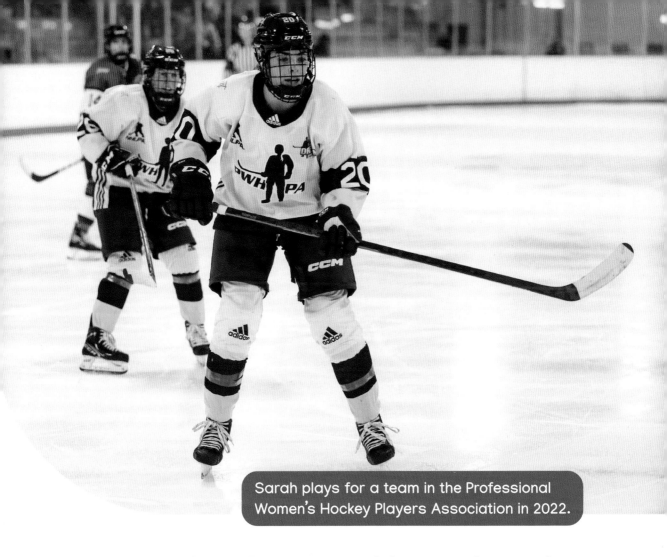

Sarah plays for a team in the Professional Women's Hockey Players Association in 2022.

In 2019, around 200 players in Canada's National Women's Hockey League took part in efforts to improve the game. They demanded to be paid. As a result, the players formed a new **association** – the Professional Women's Hockey Players Association. In 2023, a new Professional Women's Hockey League was created and Sarah was drafted to the Toronto team. In 2024, the first season began.

Now, players, fans and others involved in the game are all working hard to give women's ice hockey a boost. The future looks bright for Sarah and her teammates.

The Path to Greatness

Sporting heroes can offer us great tips on how to be faster, stronger and more skilled. And although it looks like they have superpowers, the truth is different. The greatest athletes show us that things like courage, passion and knowing when to take risks are also important. But the things that push each athlete are unique. Athletes carve their own paths to greatness, in sport and in life.

Now, go on! Walk, jump, roll, swim, skate and run your way to sporting success.

Go for it!

Who will our sporting heroes of the future be?

Glossary

adaptive surfer (*noun*)	a surfer who uses things such as special equipment or the help of a guide to make up for a disability
association (*noun*)	a group of people who have joined together for the same purpose
championships (*noun*)	contests where a final winner is decided in a sport or game
draft (*noun*)	a system in which a professional sports team chooses players each year
football scholarship (*noun*)	money given to a talented young football player to help pay for their education
funding (*noun*)	money given to a person or group for a particular purpose
guernsey (*noun*)	a type of sleeveless shirt worn by Australian Rules football players
league (*noun*)	a group of sports teams that play against each other to earn points to find which team is best
pandemic (*noun*)	when an infectious disease affects one or more countries or the whole world at one time
passion (*noun*)	a strong feeling of excitement for something
professional (*adjective*)	paid to participate in a sport or activity
racism (*noun*)	unfair treatment of people because of their race
refugees (*noun*)	people who have had to leave their country to stay safe
reserve (*noun*)	land set aside in the past for First Nations peoples to live on, not managed by the government
retired (*verb*)	stopped playing a sport, or stopped working
rights (*noun*)	things that all people deserve to have or be able to do
schedule (*noun*)	a plan for when things will be done
shot–put (*noun*)	the sport of throwing a heavy metal ball (called a shot) as far as possible
sighted guide (*noun*)	a person who helps an athlete who is visually impaired by telling them about things they cannot see
visually impaired (*adjective*)	partly or completely blind

Index